HUNGRY LADYBUGS

by Judith Jango-Cohen

PULL AHEAD BOOKS

Animals

⌐ Lerner Publications Company • Minneapolis

To my son Steven. He reminds me of the ladybug because he makes everyone smile.

This book is available in two editions:
Library binding by Lerner Publications Company, a division of Lerner Publishing Group, Inc.
Soft cover by First Avenue Editions, an imprint of Lerner Publishing Group, Inc.
241 First Avenue North
Minneapolis, MN 55401 U.S.A.

Website address: www.lernerbooks.com

Words in *italic* type are explained in a glossary on page 30.

Library of Congress Cataloging-in-Publication Data

Jango-Cohen, Judith.
   Hungry ladybugs / By Judith Jango-Cohen.
     p. cm. — (Pull ahead books)
   Summary: Describes the physical characteristics
and behavior of the insect commonly known as a
ladybug.
    ISBN-13: 978-0-8225-4667-2 (lib. bdg. : alk. paper)
    ISBN-10: 0-8225-4667-1 (lib. bdg. : alk. paper)
    ISBN-13: 978-0-8225-3646-8 (pbk. : alk. paper)
    ISBN-10: 0-8225-3646-3 (pbk. : alk. paper)
    1. Ladybugs—Juvenile literature. [1. Ladybugs.]
I. Title. II. Series.
QL596.C65 J36 2003
595.76'9—dc21   2002009440

Manufactured in the United States of America
2 3 4 5 6 7 — JR — 12 11 10 09 08 07

What *insect* is black, bumpy, hairy, and hungry?

This black, bumpy, hairy insect
is a ladybug.

It has just hatched from its egg.

A ladybug
that has just
hatched is
called a
larva.

A ladybug larva is always hunting for food.

What kind of food is this hungry larva hunting for?

Most ladybugs eat tiny insects
called *aphids*.

Aphids live on plants
like roses and wheat.

They suck the
sweet sap
from the
plant stems.

A ladybug larva uses its spiky jaws to bite an aphid.

Then it sucks out the aphid's insides.

A ladybug larva grows fast.

But only the soft inside of
a larva's body can grow.

The larva's hard outside
exoskeleton cannot.

Soon the exoskeleton
gets too tight.

Then it splits
open.

A bigger larva wriggles out.

The ladybug larva has *molted.*
It grows and molts four times.

The fourth time the ladybug molts,
it becomes a *pupa*.

The pupa does not eat.
It rests for five days.

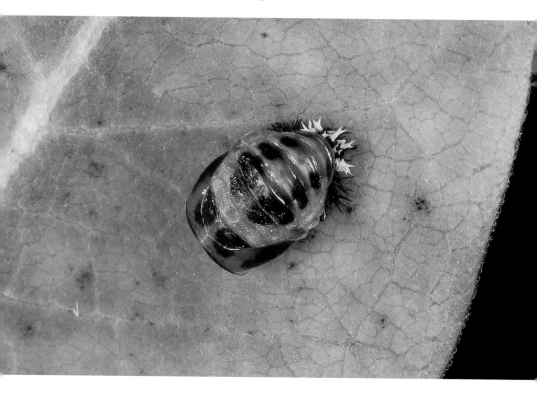

Look closely.
What is the pupa turning into?

The pupa has turned into
an *adult* ladybug.

Soon the ladybug will turn red.
Its spots will appear.

Count the legs on an adult ladybug.

Ladybugs are insects,
so they have six legs.

A ladybug is a kind of insect called a *beetle*.

Beetles have two hard wing cases. The wing cases lock together.

A ladybug can unlock its wing cases.

Do you know what will pop out?

Two long wings
are folded up inside.

The ladybug unfolds these wings
to fly.

Soon the ladybug will fly away
to find food.

What kind of food will it hunt for?

Adult ladybugs eat aphids too.

Ladybugs are *predators*. A predator hunts and eats other animals.

Ladybugs hunt for aphids
on plant stems.

Claws help
ladybugs
climb.

A frog sees
a climbing
ladybug.

The frog is a predator too.
It hunts insects.

The ladybug folds up its legs
and tucks in its head.

The frog thinks the ladybug is dead.
It leaves the ladybug alone.

A female ladybug that stays safe
will lay eggs.

She lays her tiny eggs
on a plant that has lots of aphids.

After all, the black, bumpy,
hairy hunters that hatch
will be hungry!

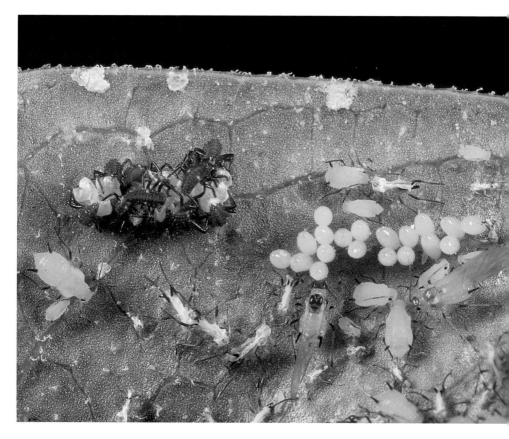

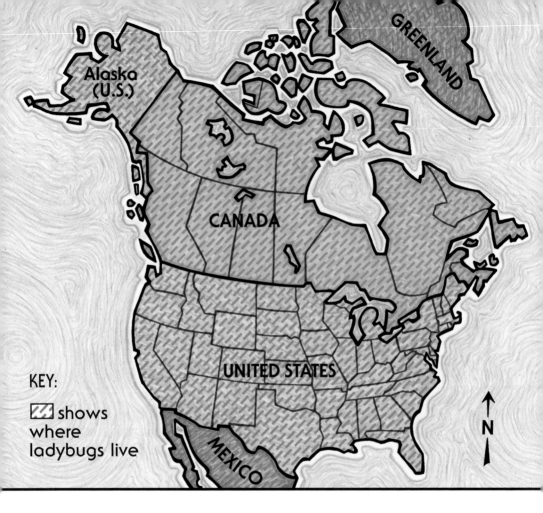

KEY:

shows where ladybugs live

Alaska (U.S.)

GREENLAND

CANADA

UNITED STATES

MEXICO

N

Find your state or province on this map.
Do ladybugs live near you?

Parts of a Ladybug's Body

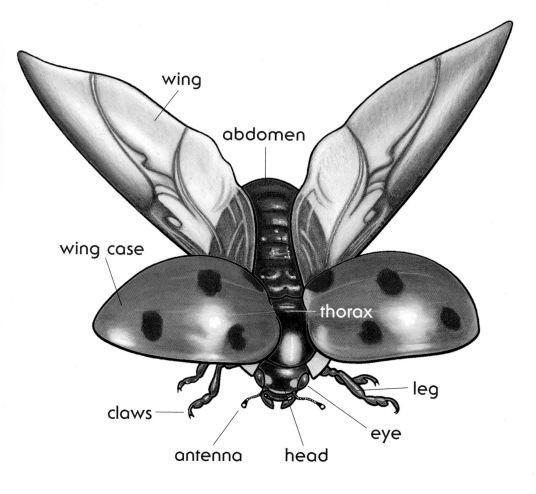

wing

abdomen

wing case

thorax

claws

leg

eye

antenna

head

Glossary

adult: a full-grown ladybug

aphid: a tiny insect that sucks the juices from plants

beetle: an insect with wing cases that protect its wings

exoskeleton: the hard outside covering of a ladybug's body

insect: an animal that has three main body parts and six legs

larva: the stage in a ladybug's life after it hatches from an egg

molt: get rid of an old, tight outer covering

predators: animals that hunt and eat other animals

pupa: the resting stage in a ladybug's life after it is a larva and before it becomes an adult

Hunt and Find

- ladybugs **eating aphids** on pages 9–11, 22, 27
- ladybug **eggs** on pages 3, 4, 5, 26, 27
- **flying** ladybugs on pages 20–21
- ladybug **larvas** on pages 3–6, 9–13, 27
- **molting** ladybugs on pages 12–16
- a ladybug **playing dead** on page 25
- ladybug **pupas** on pages 14–15

About the Author

Eliat Cohen

"When you see a ladybug you have to smile," says Judith Jango-Cohen, so she had a wonderful time researching ladybugs for this book. Her most interesting ladybug experience took place in California, where she found a clump of about one hundred ladybugs clinging to a stem. She has also found a larva taking a walk on her sweater in Maine. And in her home in Burlington, Massachusetts, she often finds ladybugs snuggled up in nooks. There is even a wooden ladybug with wiggly legs sitting on her desk and watching her work. Look around carefully. You just might find a ladybug or two sitting and watching you.

Photo Acknowledgments

The photographs in this book are reproduced with the permission of: © Robert and Linda Mitchell, front cover, 3, 9, 10, 11, 17, 18, 20, 21, 22, 23, 27; © Jerome Wexler/Visuals Unlimited, pp. 4, 5; © Bill Johnson / Visuals Unlimited, p. 6; © Richard Walters/Visuals Unlimited, p. 7; © Charles W. Melton, pp. 8, 14; © Dwight R. Kuhn, pp. 12, 13, 16, 19, 24, 31; © Scott Camazine, p. 15; © Bill Banaszewski /Visuals Unlimited, p. 25; © Peter K. Ziminski /Visuals Unlimited, p. 26.